The Cupped Field

READING DEIRDRE O'CONNOR'S POEMS can feel like watching a sunset from a darkening forest where you are not quite sure if you are lost. There is that kind of sublime in them: an intimate, luminous lyric voice acknowledging a world in which we can never be sure we are oriented as we think we are. Written with great compassion, precision, and nuance, these gorgeously made poems face into the heartbreaks of time and loss, of selves and ex-selves. They loosen vision from its nostalgias, and "shake/ the cobbled order of ground,/ so silence [can] be heard/ clearly again."

— Mary Szybist, author of *Incarnadine*

ONE OF THE SECRETS in the arts of the lyric voice is knowing what loneliness is. How to be alone and not alone at all. *The Cupped Field* is a book where lyric voice reigns. And so, it is no surprise that whether she writes about aging parents or relationships between lovers or dying of loved ones, about Greta Garbo or a deer that slammed into a car and now lies weeping on the road, Deirdre O'Connor always asks this larger question: What is the secret of our loneliness? "Loneliness is snow arriving by night,/ horseback snow, the clatter of hooves." Yes. But also: "Loneliness is a loosening/ flock of starlings over a walled city." Indeed. But then, again: "The self is winter's luxury for the alone." Absolutely. But she also sees "a serotonin bee, perhaps, a bee of loneliness."

Deirdre O'Connor is an exquisite lyric poet. Open this book on any page—perhaps open it on poems like "Déjà vu" or "On the 365th Day of the Year" and you will see it. These are not just good poems. They are spells.

How is she able to do it? Perhaps because she knows that loneliness, for a lyric poet, is not just a state of being; it comes with a purpose. What is that purpose? To hear among the "mind's countries" the music. What kind of music? That of mystery. The "mystery within trumping/ the mystery without," yes. But also the mystery of how "we lie down every night without/ having seen our kidneys, never gaze/ upon our hearts; still,/ we sleep well enough."

This mystery is the candlelit cathedral at midday inside these poems, yes. But there is also the mystery and music of a body sitting still as a body can, inside the illusion of time.

As I said, Deirdre O'Connor is an exquisite lyric poet. It is the truth.

— Ilya Kaminsky, author of *Deaf Republic*

THE CUPPED FIELD OFFERS surprising and accurate images, exquisite observations, thoughtful and deep wisdom. There are some amazing turns of empathy, as when the poet enters the pain of the distant past and of the distant present. Her poem channeling a woman in the North of Ireland—"the absence of human strife// that she was never a part of// ricocheted// amid the architecture"—brought back and clarified my own brief visit to Belfast some years ago. In the poem titled "Sunflowers," the heavy-headed flowers ". . . exude/ a crowded sorrow,/ like refugees/ at a fence. They make me/ think of backpacks/ crammed with diapers, toddlers in arms/ and eight-year-olds/ walking along . . . ," evoking a contemporary heartbreak. *The Cupped Field* shares with us the experience of loss, while also reminding us of the anniversaries we might celebrate of the days when those we love did *not* die. Here is a poet who knows that the mind is complex, a map of many countries, in some of which people are starving. The poet tells us that the mind resides in the brain, which is held in the skull, "the darkest place in the body," yet it is "buoyant inside,/ thinking it swims/ in regions beyond itself."

— Marilyn Nelson, 2018 Able Muse Book Award judge, author of
Faster Than Light: New and Selected Poems, 1996-2011

THE CUPPED FIELD REVEALS the pressure of the poet's gaze turning everything she beholds to metaphor. So often the inner and outer world collide in these poems. Painterly in quality, they reconstruct a moment to hold "the mystery within" and "the mystery without." The history of place, family, the difficulty of watching those we love die—these are just some of the subjects to which O'Connor returns. A gifted lyric poet, she frequently "unlatches us from time" so we may better comprehend the vexation of matters like memory and the mind. Yet her poems equally inhabit the present, her imagination expansive enough to encompass the politics of our time. Even when, for instance, O'Connor sits in "meditation" overlooking a seemingly pastoral landscape, her knowledge that others do not have the luxury of safety suffuses the poem.

— Shara McCallum, author of *Madwoman*

The
CUPPED
FIELD

POEMS BY

Deirdre O'Connor

WINNER OF THE 2018 ABLE MUSE BOOK AWARD

ABLE MUSE PRESS

Able Muse Press

www.ablemusepress.com

Printed in the United States of America

Library of Congress Control Number: 2019937308

ISBN 978-1-77349-035-9 (paperback)
ISBN 978-1-77349-036-6 (digital)

Cover image: "Curvature" by Matt Molloy

Cover & book design by Alexander Pepple

Able Muse Press is an imprint of *Able Muse:* A Review of Poetry, Prose & Art—at www.ablemuse.com

Able Muse Press
467 Saratoga Avenue #602
San Jose, CA 95129

For Bill

Acknowledgments

My grateful acknowledgments go to the editors of the following publications where these poems, some in earlier versions, first appeared:

American Journal of Nursing: "Déjà vu"

The Bucknell Afterword: "Death Listens without Ears to the Language I Now Speak"

Cave Wall: "Itinerary: Lahinch," "Itinerary: Site of the Former Laurelton Village for Feeble-Minded Girls of Childbearing Age," and "Archival"

Cleaver: "A Man and a Name" and "Self-Portrait as Autistic Sky"

Cordella: "Neighborhood Elegy" and "The Darkest Place"

Crazyhorse: "Relic"

Frontiers: A Journal of Women's Studies: "A Version of Her Suicide: In the North of Ireland"

Guesthouse: "On Seeing an Exhibition of Rudolf and Leopold Blaschka's Glass Marine Invertebrates"

McSweeney's Internet Tendency: "Domestic Sestina"

Natural Bridge: "Indelible Letter"

Pebble Lake Review: "If the Aspen" (as "Some Days So Far Off They May Be Today"), "The Yoke," and "Notes for those who will spend a long time watching someone die"

Xconnect: "Almost Elegy" and "Premonition"

"The Continuum" appeared in *A Slant of Light: Reflections on Jack Wheatcroft*, edited by Peter Balakian and Bruce Smith (Bucknell University Press, 2018).

"Death Listens without Ears to the Language I Now Speak" appeared in *Poems and Their Making: A Conversation*, edited by Philip Brady (Etruscan Press, 2015).

"Wake" appeared in the anthology *Mentor & Muse: Essays from Poets to Poets*, edited by Blas Falconer, Beth Martinelli, and Helena Mesa (Southern Illinois University Press, 2010).

My gratitude to Marilyn Nelson and Alex Pepple for having faith in this book. Thank you to the Vermont Studio Center and the Achill Heinrich Boll Association for residencies that allowed me to work on some of these poems. I also thank Bucknell University, especially the Writing Center, the Bucknell Seminar for Undergraduate Poets, the Stadler Center for Poetry, and the Office of the Provost.

Many thanks to those who provided feedback at various stages of this book's evolution: Peg Cronin, Bill Flack, Katie Hays, Sue Ellen Henry, Sabrina Kirby, Sandra Kohler, Laurie Kutchins, Teresa Leo, Shara McCallum, Jeanne Minahan McGinn, Ron Mohring, April Ossman, Jeff Plunkett, Steve Styers, the late Jack Wheatcroft, and Shanna Powlus Wheeler.

Gratitude also to the following for their support: E.G. Asher, Catherine Blair, Paula Closson Buck, Janice Butler, Nancy Campbell, Andy Ciotola, Nicole Cooley, Erica Delsandro, Sebastian Doherty, Gale Duque, Betse Esber, Abe Feuerstein, Will Flack, Chrissy Friedlander, Ramona Fruja, Loren Gustafson, Cynthia Hogue, Ilya Kaminsky, Ruth Ellen Kocher, Marjorie Maddox, Mike Malusis, Joe McGinn, Erica Meadows, Robert Midkiff, Megan Mulligan, Anne O'Donnell, Shane Ó Maoildhia, Kerry Ose, Diana Park, Cindy Peltier, Marjorie Priceman, Rosalyn Richards, Joe Scapellatto, Chet'la Sebree, Bruce Smith, Mary Szybist, Rhett Iseman Trull, and G.C. Waldrep. Special thanks to my family, near and far, and to all the Junies over the years.

Contents

I

(far)

II

(near)

III

(near)

IV

(far)

. . . the marble ear, in which you always speak

—Rainer Maria Rilke, *Sonnets to Orpheus*

The Cupped Field

Premonition

Loneliness is snow arriving by night,
horseback snow, the clatter of hooves

on the street and their sudden
distance. Their muting also by snow.

Rooms not thought of in years
fill with revising and silence,

a white blocking the colors
of noise. The diffuse recollected,

dust in a bin, might be mine:
ancient motes and light, hurtling matter.

I feel the black and white sounds
of near and far, the sense of a red scarf

quieted, as if the blood had been wrung from it
in a terrible wash that did not include me.

I

(far)

Itinerary: Lahinch

Today I click
among flower artists,
a still life with dead fish,

a picture of waves crashing
on the shopfronts of Lahinch.
The white roses' interior gold

vs. the scales' whitesilver,
and how the Lahinch photographer
made the water flames:

the orange light of emergency
jostling chimneys,
slapping windows and doors

beyond the promenade
where wetsuits hang on racks
like sharks.

Impossible in repose
to say how far we are
from emergency.

Years ago, a deer
slammed into my mother's car,
and afterwards it lay weeping

on the side of the road, the car
awash, she said, in glass and fur,
tears striping the face of the doe.

I shocked myself
by dropping to my knees.
Sometimes the body prays

without intending to.
Or one self sinks while the other stands
on shore, the ocean

closing over, its great rolling horses
corralled, a finger of sun
holding the horizon down.

At the Site of the Laurelton Village for Feeble-Minded Girls of Childbearing Age

No ghosts. Only witness trees
casting dark on lawns. Cool nets.

Rustles above, alongside.
Where the fields were, maybe,

green beans, cukes, tomatoes.
Where the grass now sways hip-high,

hips in cotton dresses swayed.
Where the orchards: pear, plum, apple.

Baskets of them in arms.
Where stone was lifted and made

an institution.
Porches painted white.

Can't you see the ones called morons
mending dresses,

idiots shelling peas,
the deviant

berry-pickers, water-fetchers,
milkers of cows,

and those incorrigibles
who couldn't be trusted

with a shovel,
weeding the long rain-loosened rows

on hands and knees? Scrubbing floors,
hanging sheets to flap

and then by supper
spread again on beds.

Can't you see yourself
standing inside the corn

grown higher than faces?
How you might watch the whores

and nulliparae dance
like boys and girls,

music drifting
from open windows, curtains wafting

as if in a film and you alone
in knowing what you were

missing? No one seeming to notice,
no one bashing through stalks to lead you

back by the ordinary arm.

Garbo

Greta Garbo is resting, says Manuel,
of his hemiparetic arm. She wants to be alone.
Propped on a pillow, she will not give
an interview. We have to imagine her
conveying without speech, taking her time
as she did in Södermalm in 1912,
crossing the small stone squares back from the alley
where she watched the actors arrive
and, standing outside the theatre, listened
as they spoke their lines. She could see the ships
sailing across the Strommen, the mackerel sky and sun
going down. The mystery within trumping
the mystery without. That sense of being
acted upon but felt by the self alone,
the world a stage and the body also.
The mind alive in the theatre.

A Version of Her Suicide: In the North of Ireland

She dreamt her loneliness a loosening
flock of starlings over the walled city,

and she, a girl again in hard shoes
echoing as she passed

up Waterloo, through
Butcher's Gate, and into

the city's heart. Soldiers gone,
graffiti fading, peace

more or less achieved. And yet
the absence of human strife

that she was never a part of
ricocheted

amid the architecture,
its need to escape upwards.

Maybe she wanted to shake
the cobbled order of ground,

so silence could be heard
clearly again. More than heard.

Neighborhood Elegy

Impossible to say I'll never forget the woman
across the street sinking to her knees in the yard

    all the little flags of memory
    snapping

and wailing, *I can't go on, I don't want to*
be alone, while another woman who looked like her

    as if it's easy to be seen

reached through tangled curls to knead her neck—
the way the sister figure stood stiffly bending over her

    rooted ministrations

as the woman curled downward, her forehead
on the grass, her whole body shaking

    a seizure of time

and her earthbound cries so loud I heard them
two blocks away. I had lifted my hand to my chest

    the third ear closes its eye

as if my own heart had been struck and locked
eyes with the sister for a moment. Her look

the heart attacks

betrayed no judgment of my having seen.
Her face was solemn, or neutral, and she probably

forgotten face

wouldn't remember she'd seen me stopped
then slowly jogging off, running the whole block

no clock, no loud
apologizing

before I felt my hand still raised to my chest
as if I were pledging allegiance, the spilling cries

branch to breath

persisting until I passed the school,
where the last day of classes had started,

brimming cup

and the giant oak out front that had grown over generations
marked the first quarter mile.

amid the rustle, jays

To Your Mind: Fill In the Blank

One of your mind's countries is poor and lacks
the infrastructure characteristic of most
of the hemisphere. The trees have plastic sacks
caught in their branches, rubbish that got lost
in hot wind, lifted, filled and snagged like white
flags of surrender—a bag for every mouth
starving for what such bags might contain: rice,
papayas, Coca-Cola. Local youth
scavenge the dump, pick amid smoking heaps
of tires, mosquitoes, rats, the invisible
font of disease. How do they learn to keep
your mind's miseries alive? If they could kill
you off and thereby destroy the map! The kind
who expect _____ do not live in your mind.

St. Patrick's Cathedral

The candlelit cathedral at midday:
    a heavy door falls shut,

and the bustle disappears.
    Eyes adjust to shadows

amid the stone and winter coats,
    the click and echo of heels

a young woman apologizes for.
    A candle costs two dollars:

the going rate for one among the many
    clustered flames: can the cost

of suffering ever be qualified?
    A man in a plaid jacket stands erect

before Our Lady of Guadalupe.
    Eyes closed, hands clasped, he might be

Nicaraguan, Salvadoran;
    might be reverent, desperate, both.

Impossible to know that kind of privacy,
    or even to encroach on it,

here where admiration and whispering
    are permitted. The Pietà has so different

a beauty from the actual women here,
    though each would carry a sacrifice

in her arms, or already does, invisibly,
    and each must startle occasionally

with grace in the presence of hatred,
    the way so many women do

growing old. They kneel and lower their heads
    in the posture of those who imagine

better lives for other people,
    and they are the ones whose faces

most resemble alcove saints,
    the peripheral ones in stations

along the walls in semidarkness
    where a teenage boy—

far from the many wars
    of the moment—

stops to study each of them,
    then moves on.

Sunflowers

A disarray of sunflowers in the field
  outside town. Some hang their heads,

    look askance at the land
  that will become

their graves. They exude
  a crowded sorrow,

    like refugees
  at a fence. They make me

think of backpacks
  crammed with diapers,

    toddlers in arms
  and eight-year-olds

walking along.
  Hoodies, fleeces,

    veils, how American
  they seem, or fail to seem.

So much depends upon
  where we are taken,

    what, given the climate, we expect.
  Now the evening light

flows over and through
     the tops of trees. Weightless,

          traveling like an idea
     of money, its cinematic gold

brightens land
     people think they own.

          So often nostalgia is tinted
     the color of urine,

so often a top-heavy flower
     nods like a person,

          blooming or stiffened,
     seeming to do all it can

to last. And then when it goes,
     it goes

          quietly, under the kind of arrest
     we saw coming

all over the planet.

Self-Portrait as Autistic Sky

Nothing I can name, but in perception
there's spinning. Stimuli in the distances:

suns, planets, moons, cosmic rocks
in transit. Sometimes, almost palpable, blue goes gray;

blue black; black blacker; all the shades of white
go away. The silvers and the lightning

may be forked attempts to reach,
successful feathers.

Precipitation flows through:
much is that transparent, needling.

Some look up to understand,
but I am not horizon-bound.

I do not presume (like looking up words)
there is a book,

though maybe there are boundaries, pages
maybe, something to say it on like me.

II

(near)

Meditation in Lewisburg, Pennsylvania

The self obscures the self as light
  carves a day loose from time,
    chisels it to a random April fifth,
  four o'clock shadows

pointing east, a few rain-scattered leaves
  drying flat as handprints. I'm behind a window
    watching the mostly leafless oaks
  just stand (that's all I see them doing).

The grass has lost its winter blond.
  I in my chair sit still as a body can
    inside the illusion of time. My eyes
  rake the scene free of what I think

it attaches to me, this now,
  no, *this* now,
    which, when I write it down,
  becomes *this snow,*

this snow, a way of covering things,
  the ethical problem,
    privilege of saying, *I am here*
  in this calm place

while elsewhere girls are being stacked
  in trucks, cast off in flimsy rafts,
    and my primary terror
  is only death.

A Man and a Name

A man screws a woman, then is smitten
    by another with her name.

        He is like the sky's coincidence,
    never the same cumulonimbi,

but always the sky. He is in the look
    of the gift horse, the whites of the horse's eyes.

        Together, the man and the woman
    inhabit a certain reddish gray

like hydrangea dust in lace at an inn
    they might have visited;

        apart, they live
    the finest distinctions,

the first-name basis of difference,
    which hates what it might love.

        A name is a tool, after all,
    a strategy, not a hat rack,

though both have cursive elements,
    branches and hooks.

Even a name, like desire, can be owned
not at all. Braid against better wishes.

The self is winter's luxury for the alone.

Almost Elegy

I.

His slit wrists wrapped like little mummies,
I sat on the edge of the bed and held his hand
and made myself kiss his hair like a mother
then kissed his eyebrows and nose.
Until that afternoon I'd been my mother
when she was young, expecting a man
to draw me out of darkness, a fish
to whom a crumb is tossed.

Imagine from underneath the shining surface
of the pond, the silver brilliance
nearing. Swimming up and up.
You know it, too, the cold-to-warm,
the hollow knocking sound of oars,
the smooth blue-bottomed boat
that grows so huge you lose the sky.
Then the shred of bread, the unseen
hand that dropped it, all too human.

II.

To wish you happy birthday, a note. I hope
this May finds you buff and vexatiously graying
beneath Denali, where I picture you in a taupe
living room scattered with Indian pillows and fraying
rugs, dark blues and reds, like veins and blood
all these years unspilled. Since when did our shared grief
split like fixable conjoined twins and hood-
wink memory of the one life worth leaving?
I remember cutting your hair on the porch, the just-
washed scent of your hair and aftershaved jaw, the smoke
of a football cookout nearby, and the acrid dust
of something not meant to burn registered. I woke
to my own awakeness, perhaps, there in the plain
act of cutting something that couldn't hurt, beautiful hair.

Indelible Letter

But now I am tired as oceans, and seeing
what oceans see: gray mirror skies and clouds
both empty and full, if clouds, like mothers, might be said
to contain. I am lace-edged, variable, cool; sluiced
through, plummeted, swum; closing and open.
You play on the beach of me and would bury
yourself, if you could. Your shovel and green pail
float; the shells you've gathered sink. I would carry them
on my tongue if I need not speak. Your father in you
is a banned continent, a map without land. Never
a bridge, never a means to an end, merely the end—
its language, color, line. To erase the place (the idea,
the representation) we may not go (I must include you).

Rock and Hard Place

At first just puddles seemed rained upon,
as if the ground were simmering,
and then the sky let loose
its pent-up bells.

The hush was loud. A girl
got drenched in seconds and kept running
along the path beneath the trees.
Somewhere to get to.

Not like me, or me with you.
We were still as portraits
even before we met, and could have stood
in a rainswept place

as statues on a hill.
We'd have shown a stone look
as the helpless river filled,
ourselves outlasted.

Reprieve

January fifth: the cold snap breaks, or opens:
a spinachy smell of pigshit drifts in the air
above the white yard, the cut corn poking up
in the white fields. Beyond them, more fields
and the slick road snow is falling on, houses,
town, the prison, schools, cities, edges, oceans.
A woman proceeds carefully down the steps
to the gravel drive, to the carport where the car is
lightly shrouded in snow, as if it had died overnight
and she must lift the sheet. But the engine starts as it must,
and it must because she's alone for reasons infinite
as snow, infinite as fear, fear of the trivial
fears that mutate into symbols, fear of the voice
that asks for help and the help being useless.
But the engine starts, the windshield's wiped,
and the road seems clear enough to disappear on.

We Must Become Our Own Mothers and Fathers

Hope as vertigo, a high optimism
that shouldn't look down,

as when one rushes to comfort
a sobbing child.

The flushed cheeks are beautiful
sheeted with tears,

because comfort is believed
by someone taller.

Comfort is believed
so hope outlasts.

Someone has to embrace,
to dry the damp face,

warm, shirted flesh
pressing against

the teary lashes,
the eyes by some inarticulate

feeling or seeing
blurred in their purpose,

closed with and against.

The Darkest Place

We lie down every night without
    having seen our kidneys, never gaze

        upon our hearts; still,
    we sleep well enough. Despite atrophy

here and there, our organs pulse,
    a nest of rabbits. Our pinks brown,

        streaked with fat.
    Given the skull, the brain must be

the darkest place
    in the body, though the mind

        craves light, motion,
    the sensation of roving

while being contained. Held, fed.
    Brain as mother, brain as ocean

        rising, falling, the mind
    buoyant inside,

thinking it swims
    in regions beyond itself.

Domestic Sestina

As usual, falling asleep she pictured a hill and upon the hill a house.
She could not anticipate too much, had to let them form in her mind,
and then in her mind walk up the hill, and then open the door.
Sometimes the hill was in Japan, sometimes Latin America,
often Ireland or France. She could tell the country by the coins
in her pocket, though sometimes there were elaborate gardens

suggesting a national character, a preponderance of gardens
leading up to or extending behind the house,
sometimes a fountain beneath which greenish tile glinted with coins
scattered across the bottom, fees for the mind's
dreaming. Always she forgot she had fallen asleep in America,
far from the village roads lined with bombs, the opening doors

of ruin. She believed inside the heart there was a door
unlocked by beauty. Here were the white gravel gardens
raked daily by monks, here were the ponds far from America
stocked with koi that gleam and leap, here was the tea house
shaded by banana and palm, by evergreen and the mind
of winter and plum blossoms falling like silent coins

to carpet a new geography. Maybe like blossoms the coins
grew on trees, maybe the silvers and coppers were the only doors
in the world? She had to believe the ideas her mind
delivered at night, when she was asleep in ancestral gardens
scented by lilac and pear, when she was the dark house
herself filled with ghosts long ago called to America.

Asleep, she never wondered why anyone came to America.
Of course, the streets were paved with gold, and buckets of coins
were rainbow luck, and every family had its house
with curtains and swings and a slot in the door
through which letters and checks were deposited. Even the gardens
were ripe for those who did not mind

too much being given. But it was not only her dreaming mind
that wished to live in the kind of house
she'd always imagined; it was the houses and gardens
themselves insisting they be desired. True, there were coins
jingling in her pockets, enough, but nowhere would she find a door
to such desires, never would the stones leading up to the house

through fragrant gardens transplant her as routinely as her mind
to her mind's houses, even the musty, foursquare American
houses, common as coins, keys still hung by the door.

Wake

The longing of heavy blankets that weigh
        upon sleeping bodies, selves removed
                to interiors

finite as the hours. I hear the bleat of lambs
        being shorn, the squelch and muck of fields,
                the hands' grasp of tools.

The distance between blades and flesh:
        the imagining mind at rest, eyes rolled back
                in sockets, breathing steady except

for occasional gasps of terror. Dreams
        that dissipate faster than smoke
                never so slowly evaporate

as puddles indelicately stepped in
        or a glass of water left bedside
                in the guest room where no one has

counted sheep in months. The house appears
        to want nothing but to be entered
                and kept, inhabited as by fingers

in a cast-off, reclaimed glove, and the beds inside
        are clean and empty-cool as silence
                where a bloodless battle had been.

Notes from the Periphery

The towels are thin and rough and smell
like cigarettes. Smokers had to have gathered
where they dried. Maybe just one, inhaling,

exhaling, the smoke an exact color match
to the fog, the cigarette white like the sky.
The sky is the same everywhere. It can't

ever be captured the way smoke can be
caught in a jar or stiff towels hastily folded
and stacked, retaining the washed stain

of strangers, their breath. Strangers fill with smoke,
and the places they travel echo their smells,
the drab bits they leave behind, broken

pens, trial-sized shampoos, strands
of dark hair sticking to soap
flattened on the sink's western edge.

III

(near)

The Yoke

"Open thy mouth wide, and I will fill it," reads the needlepoint
above the dentist's door, beyond which "Little Learners"
are doing time in the chair. One at a time, up and down,
they practice how to be not afraid, to tip their chins,
spit. And then to brush in circles gently
for two minutes. No blood today, no needles, drills,
just a plastic sack of gifts: a magnet of a happy tooth,
a purple toothbrush, paste. In the waiting room,
their winter coats are stacked: smooth, inflatable animals,
an occasional Pittsburgh Steeler in the mix.
The youngest ones need help getting their arms in,
getting zipped, and when they're all lined up and holding
hands in pairs, they lift their faces as if toward God
to the camera. Having been happily trained for pain,
they flash their unharmed smiles, and in my mind, I exit
with them, all my ex-selves, mittens attached
to their jackets, bright and unbreakable.

If the Aspen

If the quaking aspen could take a soul,
      it would take my mother's, *Populus tremuloides*

absorbing *paralysis agitans*,
      and the pile of sawdust steaming in earliest sun

would take my father's, everything he's sheltered
      along with everything

he's harmed. This road would accommodate
      both of them, the edges and hills of the road

that passes the lumber mill and its machines,
      the belts that turn like bracelets and grip

the wrists of logs, the ribs and hips and knees,
      and feed them to the teeth . . .

There are no burials here, unless some of the perfect
      planks end up as coffins lowered

across the Lamoille. Some of the planks come back, perhaps,
      reunited with an acre, the family

building a house overlooking Dog's Head Falls,
      the worker in dungarees who builds a table

from throwaway wood and carries back in his hair
      the transubstantiated dust.

Loosening Masonry

A bird hit the living room window

    while her father was talking

        and later she dreamt an owl arrived

    from the sea with the baby's face.

The baby's face was her father's,

    and the sea was the land

        beyond the window, the open

    November fields of cut-down corn.

Shorn, the sea, to a stubbled page.

    As if to be read, a phrase swooped up

        from the rough book of the field: "loosening

masonry." Like the house someday

whose window was met by the bird.

Loosening now, the fields, the sea,

      her father seeing stars through a cold telescope

on the porch, the power of glass.

Anniversary: One of the Days My Mother Did Not Die

The day after my rained-on wedding, the sky
was a desert, blank and hot. Beneath the tent

in our friend's backyard were candles
to be gathered, vases, linens, ring-bearer pillows.

My husband and I rinsed the caterer's plates
to get the discount. So many plates stacked with remains

of dinner we didn't eat greeting the guests—
salmon, pesto, lettuce, even the violets from the cake.

The hose's leaky nozzle made a rainbow
and ruined my shoes. There in the sweat and muck,

penny-saving, stacking chairs, my husband rolling tables
across the wrecked lawn, I could not feel my mother

sail her Acura up and over the shoulder of Route 22,
flattening road signs one two three before

she finally stopped, scarring a tree or two,
and then was lifted loose

with just a lump on her leg, some cuts and glass
in her hair, my mother opening the heart of death

to see what makes it tick, to watch it work
as machinery works, as hands and eyelids work,

or love—any of the miracles—then sewing it up,
rag doll ghost, a year ago, August first.

Portrait of Him among Bees

The only child, he felt alone among the others,
so he reddened, clenched and spit a bee up from his gut.
A serotonin bee, perhaps, a bee of loneliness
amid imagined playground flowers, red tulips
along a wall and bee-like dandelions, not alone.
Then mandible bees with wings and words like *thorax*,
words like *honey*. Bees of jaws and teeth, of language
stinging lips. Pouting bees, hissing bees, timeout bees,
Gameboy bees. Penis bees, asshole bees, posture bees,
arms-crossed bees. Bee of Mom, bee of Dad, backpack bee,
bee of the road. Homework bees, Christmas bees,
bees of extra presents. Wedding bees, stepmom bees,
limits bees, grow up bees. The child's face, a swarm of bees.

Déjà vu

So I will have written it before, I write

my mother died. It isn't true. She lives

in Pittsburgh, has a dresser, bed and chair

in her room, a wardrobe and TV.

Her name is Sharpied in all her collars

and on the inner soles of her shoes,

one of which was discovered

beneath her neighbor Mildred's pillow,

where she may have laid it down to sleep.

Blue leather shoe she wore to work

with corduroy slacks and cotton shirts,

islanded shoe, exhausted shoe

laid to rest then made to do its job

upon a foot again. Dear clairvoyant shoe,

dear keeper of an alphabet of bones, I try

to walk in you as I write my mother dies.

Aunt's Lullaby

Behind my eyes, I fall asleep seeing
my nephews, my twenty months niece, her hair
clipped away from her face like Pebbles Flintstone's,
her high forehead packed with intelligence. I see
their stocky walks, their shoes that light like robots,
their miniature Frankenstein steps, their fine pale
hair and eyes, the eyes of my sister and brother,
our mother's eyes. The baby says the sheep says,
Baa baa, and I applaud. His brother declares,
My grown-ups hardly ever cook, and *That looks
dangerous*, meaning the pool. He's the one
who asks, *When we die, will our house die, too?*,
as if he senses trees impatient to reclaim the lot,
or some shelter in our eyes beginning to smolder.

Notes for Those Who Will Spend a Long Time
Watching Someone Die

You may find yourself flying over the earth
like a child in a dream.
Or, more accurately, pulled to a great height,
grabbed and lifted and given
a view of treetops.

A kind of invisible hand
may reach through your sternum
and scoop something loose: weightless
gravel poured from the idea of a spoon
that creates an illusion of space

in your chest, an emptiness
disguised as cold stone rooms,
windows framing fields that drop dramatically
to the sea—imagination, like illness,
varies from person to person,

and time, intimate now, contracts
and expands like a finger inside a ring.
No: time,
less a finger than a ring, less a noose
than a throat, fits nothing.

The Continuum

Leaves from old oaks float
to the ground.

They smell of last October
and the next,

when you'll be dead.

*

I tell you the Cubs just won
the World Series.

Comprehension,
a few dry leaves,

tightens your gaze.

*

A few leaves scuttle
across my gaze.

I tell myself I
comprehend time

by light,
how it honeys,

deepens, feeds, dilutes,
parches, pisses on, wrecks.

To have been alive when X.
Before X.

The body its own latitude
the mind expands
until X.

*

Jack, when does time stop
holding a person?

The continuum must
fluctuate, drop

a second
here and there,

minutes, hours,

or does it buckle?

*

When I say *safe*
in their alabaster chambers,

you turn toward me as if
a star were confined into a tomb.

Relic

A sleeveless wind pretends it's summer. Despite

its caravan of geese, the sky plays along,

clean blue, just washed. A pink rose

blooms amid yellow leaves. Though I could not

fully wake you today, you said my name

with your voice. *Oh there you are*, you

said, as if you had opened your eyes,

which allowed me to take from the day

the kind of bone you'd have wanted

to throw me. The kind of bone a person

strings around her throat, even though

she might as well give it to a dog.

Death Listens without Ears to the Language I
Now Speak

This morning, the clatter of sparrows building
a nest in the air conditioner hauled upstairs
so you wouldn't suffer
the heat.

The velveteen chair I used to block
your access to the stairs
languishing, ever ugly, in the corner.

The comforter and pillows that retain invisible
strands of your DNA.

Your view from the window where one sparrow stayed
though I tapped then banged on the glass.

Death is the nest you built in my world.

Flannel threads, fringe from a scarf, fine white hairs
from the brush that last touched
your living head.

The work of a sparrow softens
the innards of a machine.

I once saw an octopus open a jar, a crow
use a lid as a sled to slide down
a metal roof.

Death is a tool
every animal invents.

I make a cage
for your exile and lower it over the world.

IV

(far)

Say the Mind

Say the mind is an ocean that passes continually
through a sieve, and what remains—the rhetorical triangle,
'i' before 'e,' memory of a brown plaid dress, etc.—
is contained in a bottle of bone the mind can't see through.
Or say the mind is a closet stuffed with your mother's clothes,
two catcher's mitts, a box of toy cars, the letters a great-uncle sent
home from the war. Leftovers like the plastic bin
of flashcards—*ubiquitous, odious, plethora*—that briefly
seem like beacons or white shirts on a tongue of land.
Say the mind is a series of points on the journey of a beast
toward extinction, the journey of a throat toward the speechless
hoard of grief. That mind is an island, and you its only inhabitant.
Its knowledge—*your* knowledge—flies randomly over the waves.

On the 365th Day of the Year

Close your eyes. This is meant to be read
to you by a child you do not know exists.
Ah, you do not follow instructions. Your eyes
move carelessly sometimes. Play a game,
shall we? I will ask a question, and the sound
of rain will begin in ears you do not know
you have. Listen. Listen to how the rain
quiets a moment before it grows loud.
But did I ask a question? I did not until
just now. And yet you leapt ahead like a child
who could not wait for the game to begin.
Now, press your hands over your ears.
Press until in your hands you hear your heart.
Now allow the rain in its infinity to return.

The Future

The clocks chose not to intervene.
      The future kept arriving. Always,
            the hours chiming in churches and schools,
      a miniscule ticking on wrists and walls.

The future kept arriving, always
      disheveled, punctual, plain
            to the chiming hours, to churches and schools,
      but odder, perhaps, than expected,

plainly disheveled, but punctual
      and carrying no bags, a surprise to those
            odd few who perhaps expected
      to depend on the past

carrying forth its baggage, but no surprise to those
      wholly grounded in the present
            who in the past depended
      on ignoring it, despite the clock's intervening.

Archival

Like rain to ice, the ancestral. All becoming,

contracted to archive. How much easier it was

to die then, to lie down and not wake up, lungs filled

to collapse, bedside tea gone cold, and the oldest

daughter finding the body warm and harried-looking

still, a ruddy mask, hands already waxen

that had an hour earlier filled a pot

with water. What is the word for not having been

in the room, for missing the turn? Should there not be

softening in every window? Snow, an oak

for the unfastening? Every girl in braids,

her chin uplifted, understudies an earlier girl.

How to convene the territories, invite the future

forward with the same indelible dark hair?

Notes on My Death

My death may resemble the koans I don't understand
     or the mundane paradox of weather, like too much
          torrential rain suddenly ending a drought,
     flash floods knocking the objects of living rooms loose—
end tables, baskets, lamps afloat—and couches
     soaked as if the earth bled upward,
          though, in fact, the rain came down.

My death may welcome a hundred cut flowers
     to my town, though I—if I were not I—might wish
          to let them live. It's a peculiar process,
figuring what I'll want when I'm dead, as if my special
     self-knowledge should translate into something,
          a dictionary to cross the space-time continuum,
     a raft of wish to break the language barrier.

My death may deliberate whether it's better
     fast or slow, duration of seedling to sapling,
          perhaps hypogeal, ghost shoot turning green
     above ground, symptoms emerging in adequate time
to count like cotyledons, to diagnose tendrils, roots,
     and study, with a novice's zeal,
          its life span, as long as it lasts.

A wafting pin oak leaf

somehow resembles
        a praying mantis—

angles spinning, leggy
        until it lands, brittle curl.

None of the urgency of the mantis,
        no menace. Stillness undoes the rhyme.

The absence of a face
        in the place it was expected, the lack

of limbs, agency, so many things missing
        it seems absurd to compare.

Possibly this is how living seems
        to the newly dead. The act of lifting an arm,

flicking hair away from a face—
        foiled, blocked—even thinking,

wingless, breathless,
        the kite it was.

The Burden

The first snowflake drops

    from the cloud. More follow.

        Droves of hexagons

    feathered and plumped,

gaining mass as they fall,

    careen, skirt sideways—

        swirl of the miniscule

    inside the vast. Like Gabriel Conroy

in the mind of Joyce and now

    in mine, snow falling

        faintly, obliquely

    over the fields, the black

branches of trees

    that meet the snow

and hold some of it

aloft, the burden

they seem to welcome.

Fractals of their sturdy

font disappear,

text, memory.

What I studied when I was young

feels like twigs nippled with ice.

By dendrites, the universe hangs.

Ballycastle Meditation

1.

Fog obscures Scotland.
> Even the near island

>> vague, green top,
> chalk cliffs

under wraps.
> Like childhood now,

>> someone else's,
> whittled, wooled.

2.

>> Memory as sheep
> chewing to nub

a cupped field.
> Memory as teeth

>> in the green, work
> against hunger, jaws.

3.

We stopped here once
    on a bus,

        you well enough to travel
    beside me.

Later, a seal in a harbor
    met your gaze

        while you stood a long time
    in a car park

lapped by ocean, dusk silking
    around you, shreds of fog,

        black water closing over
    the head of the seal

which emerged elsewhere
    again and again

        before we had to go.

4.

Elsewhere: alive.
    Nowhere: dead.

5.

         Memory lingers
   over the water,

over the field—
     wet velvet,

        a few huge glacial erratics
   cast here from afar.

Erratic from *errare*,
     to wander, go astray,

        be wrong: the gaze
   unlatched from time.

6.

Memory is the cupped field
     studded with sheep

        seen from above,
   larvae eating the cloth

of the earth,
     eating the earth alive.

On Seeing an Exhibition of Rudolf and Leopold Blaschka's Glass Marine Invertebrates

1.

From Bohemia to the deep:
      filament, tentacle crown, the creep

            toward clarity of ultramarine,
      the eyelid-purple in-between

of a fringed lamp—what is it?—
      floating in the case as if lit

            from within. Radiolaria
needle the air. Carinaria

hangs in dotted swiss.
      The octopus gazes towards us

            beyond the glass.

2.

There is no feeling of wetness
when one is below the surface,

     wrote Zarh Pritchard, who dove
        and held his breath to sketch

     on oiled paper dim veils
and shadows, coral

     sediments, fronds,
        the undulating pastel

     haze of weeds and creatures,
his pale hands quick

     with the crayon,
        everything shifting

     in slow light,
everything old, new,

     everything new, dissolving.

3.

There is a feeling of dryness
when one is strolling

instead of flowing
through a museum—

a feeling that time is being
hurried along,

there are too many corners,
there is no depth—

though anemones wave
and jellyfish rise

like lungs in darkened boxes.

DEIRDRE O'CONNOR's first book, *Before the Blue Hour*, received the Cleveland State Poetry Center Prize. Her work has appeared in *Poetry, Crazyhorse, Cave Wall*, and other journals, and she has been awarded residencies at the Vermont Studio Center and the Heinrich Boll Cottage in Ireland. She directs the Writing Center at Bucknell University, where she also serves as Associate Director of the Bucknell Seminar for Undergraduate Poets. A native of Pittsburgh, she lives in Central Pennsylvania.

ALSO FROM ABLE MUSE PRESS

Jacob M. Appel, *The Cynic in Extremis – Poems*

William Baer, *Times Square and Other Stories;*
   New Jersey Noir – A Novel;
   New Jersey Noir: Cape May – A Novel

Lee Harlin Bahan, *A Year of Mourning (Petrarch) – Translation*

Melissa Balmain, *Walking in on People (Able Muse Book Award for Poetry)*

Ben Berman, *Strange Borderlands – Poems;*
   Figuring in the Figure – Poems

Lorna Knowles Blake, *Green Hill (Able Muse Book Award for Poetry)*

Michael Cantor, *Life in the Second Circle – Poems*

Catherine Chandler, *Lines of Flight – Poems*

William Conelly, *Uncontested Grounds – Poems*

Maryann Corbett, *Credo for the Checkout Line in Winter – Poems;*
   Street View – Poems

John Philip Drury, *Sea Level Rising – Poems*

Rhina P. Espaillat, *And After All – Poems*

Anna M. Evans, *Under Dark Waters: Surviving the* Titanic *– Poems*

D. R. Goodman, *Greed: A Confession – Poems*

Margaret Ann Griffiths, *Grasshopper – The Poetry of M A Griffiths*

Katie Hartsock, *Bed of Impatiens – Poems*

Elise Hempel, *Second Rain – Poems*

Jan D. Hodge, *Taking Shape – Carmina figurata;*
   The Bard & Scheherazade Keep Company – Poems

Ellen Kaufman, *House Music – Poems*

Emily Leithauser, *The Borrowed World (Able Muse Book Award for Poetry)*

Hailey Leithauser, *Saint Worm – Poems*

Carol Light, *Heaven from Steam – Poems*

Kate Light, *Character Shoes – Poems*

April Lindner, *This Bed Our Bodies Shaped – Poems*

Martin McGovern, *Bad Fame – Poems*

Jeredith Merrin, *Cup – Poems*

Richard Moore, *Selected Poems;*
   The Rule That Liberates: An Expanded Edition – Selected Essays

Richard Newman, *All the Wasted Beauty of the World* – *Poems*

Alfred Nicol, *Animal Psalms* – *Poems*

Frank Osen, *Virtue, Big as Sin (Able Muse Book Award for Poetry)*

Alexander Pepple (Editor), *Able Muse Anthology;*
    Able Muse – a review of poetry, prose & art (semiannual, winter 2010 on)

James Pollock, *Sailing to Babylon* – *Poems*

Aaron Poochigian, *The Cosmic Purr* – *Poems;*
    Manhattanite (Able Muse Book Award for Poetry)

Tatiana Forero Puerta, *Cleaning the Ghost Room* – *Poems*

Jennifer Reeser, *Indigenous* – *Poems*

John Ridland, *Sir Gawain and the Green Knight (Anonymous)* – *Translation;*
    Pearl (Anonymous) – *Translation*

Stephen Scaer, *Pumpkin Chucking* – *Poems*

Hollis Seamon, *Corporeality* – *Stories*

Ed Shacklee, *The Blind Loon: A Bestiary*

Carrie Shipers, *Cause for Concern (Able Muse Book Award for Poetry)*

Matthew Buckley Smith, *Dirge for an Imaginary World*
    (Able Muse Book Award for Poetry)

Susan de Sola, *Frozen Charlotte* – *Poems*

Barbara Ellen Sorensen, *Compositions of the Dead Playing Flutes* – *Poems*

Rebecca Starks, *Time Is Always Now* – *Poems*

Sally Thomas, *Motherland* – *Poems*

Rosemerry Wahtola Trommer, *Naked for Tea* – *Poems*

Wendy Videlock, *Slingshots and Love Plums* – *Poems;*
    The Dark Gnu and Other Poems;
    Nevertheless – *Poems*

Richard Wakefield, *A Vertical Mile* – *Poems*

Gail White, *Asperity Street* – *Poems*

Chelsea Woodard, *Vellum* – *Poems*

www.ablemusepress.com